CLASSIC DIESEL YEARS
PERTH TO INVERNESS
TOM HEAVYSIDE

Countless spectacular views are to be enjoyed when travelling the route, such as along Strathdearn from above the River Findhorn, near Tomatin. Here, a Class 47 strides across the viaduct with the 07.06 from Edinburgh to Inverness on 12 July 1984.

© Tom Heavyside, 2022
First published in the United Kingdom, 2022,
by Stenlake Publishing Ltd.
www.stenlake.co.uk
ISBN 978-1-84033-926-0

Printed by
P2D Books, 1 Newlands Rd,
Westoning, Bedford MK45 5LD

Acknowledgements

My sincere thanks are due to Paul Abell, Bill Johnson, Ian McLean and Paul Shannon for their ready assistance in the completion of this volume. Tribute should also be expressed to all who over the years have helped revive and maintain the Strathspey Railway between Aviemore and Broomhill, where preserved steam and diesel locomotives can regularly be seen at work.

The publishers regret that they cannot supply copies of any pictures featured in this book.

Class 47 No. 47412 hurries south from Newtonmore, bound for Edinburgh with the 16.30 from Inverness, on 10 July 1984.

Introduction

From the 'Fair City' of Perth to the 'Highland Capital' of Inverness is a distance of 118 miles by rail. Threading its way through the central Highlands of Scotland, the line is undoubtedly one of the most scenic railway journeys in Britain.

The line came about piecemeal. The initial seven miles from Perth to Stanley Junction utilise metals laid by the Scottish Midland Junction Railway, which opened to Forfar on 4 August 1848. The next eight and a half miles north were promoted by the Perth & Dunkeld Railway with services commencing on 7 April 1856. Then in July 1861 the Inverness & Perth Junction Railway was authorised to build 104 miles of track between Dunkeld and Forres, to connect at the latter with the Inverness & Aberdeen Junction Railway. It was opened throughout on 9 September 1863. The following year, on 28 February, the Perth & Dunkeld was taken over by the Inverness & Perth Junction Railway.

The Inverness & Perth Junction and the Inverness & Aberdeen Junction railways merged on 1 February 1865 and became officially known as the Highland Railway from 29 June of that year. The more direct route between Aviemore and Inverness via Carrbridge opened on 1 November 1898; this was constructed by the Highland Railway and shortened the journey from Perth by twenty-six miles compared to the Forres route. Meanwhile the track south of Stanley Junction remained in other hands, becoming part of the extensive Caledonian Railway from 10 August 1866. Following the Grouping of the railways in 1923 all the lines in question became owned by the London Midland & Scottish Railway, prior to Nationalisation in 1948.

During the early years of British Railways steam remained the sole form of motive power on the line north to Inverness, but its monopoly came under increasing threat following the publication of the BR Modernisation Plan in 1955. This decreed that steam locomotives should be phased out and replaced by diesel or electric traction. Diesels first made their appearance beyond Perth in 1958 and by the summer of 1962 had taken full command of services in the Northern Division of the Scottish Region.

Despite the investment in diesel traction, in 1963 the Highland communities anxiously awaited the findings of the Beeching Report into the future of the rail network. Some feared the difficult-to-operate and sparsely populated route between Perth and Inverness would be among those slated for closure, but to the relief of many – although sadly for those affected – it was only the local services that were doomed. As a result the doors at eleven intermediate stations were locked for the last time in 1965, adding to the three that had closed during the 1950s. Further economies resulted from the closing of some signal boxes and passing loops, as well as the July 1966 singling of the previously double-track twenty-four mile section between Blair Atholl and Dalwhinnie. The four miles between Daviot and Culloden Moor were also singled in March 1968, although the double track north of Blair Atholl to Dalwhinnie was restored in April 1978.

It was in June 1980 that I first ventured north of Perth and I have been captivated – to say the least – by the Highlands ever since. This volume concentrates on the BR years from 1980 until 1993 and many would say these were the classic diesel years before Privatisation of the railways and the advent of the various multiple-units that have plied their trade between Perth and Inverness in more recent times. In contrast, a brief look is also taken at the heritage Strathspey Railway which keeps alive the spirit of past transport eras, both steam and diesel, in the Highlands.

An ornate drinking fountain on the up platform at Pitlochry, seen here on 10 July 1986.

Tom Heavyside
Bolton, Lancashire
March, 2022

Opposite: A throwback to the days of yore: Stanier Class 5 4-6-0 No. 44767 *George Stephenson* departs Perth with a returning special to Falkirk on a very wet 13 April 1985. Built by the LMS at Crewe in December 1947, it was the only one of the 842-strong class to be fitted with Stephenson link motion. It was retired by BR from Carlisle Kingmoor shed in December 1967 and is one of eighteen 'Black 5s' that have been preserved. When the class was first introduced in the summer of 1934, Nos. 5020 to 5029 were allocated new to Perth and the class became the mainstay of services over the line to Inverness until the early 1960s. In August 1950 no less than seventy-five 'Black 5s' were based at Perth shed, with a further thirty-three at Inverness and one at Aviemore. In April 1965, near the end of BR steam in Scotland and after it had been banished from the Highlands, Perth still retained a stud of twenty-five for duties in other directions.

Below: English Electric Class 37s were a more regular type of motive power to be seen at Perth during the 1980s, a total of 309 of these reliable machines having entered service between December 1960 and November 1965. Here, No. 37260 *Radio Highland* (numbered D6960 when built in January 1965) leaves southbound with a mixed freight from Inverness on 10 July 1989. Although looking quite healthy at the time, the loco was withdrawn two months later; unlike its steam counterpart, there was to be no reprieve and it was cut-up in August 1991.

Class 47 No. 47401 *North Eastern* – the prototype Brush Type 4 released from the maker's Loughborough factory as No. D1500 in September 1962 – bides time under the overall roof at Perth with the 13.22 Edinburgh Waverley to Inverness service on 3 October 1983. As befitting its status as the pioneer of a class that eventually totalled 512, after a career spanning thirty years with British Railways, No. 47401 was saved from an ignominious end in a scrapyard and today is cared for at the Midland Railway – Butterley in Derbyshire.

Sister Class 47 No. 47426 (formerly No. D1534) leaves Perth with the 09.25 from Edinburgh to Inverness on 13 April 1985. The tower that rises above Perth station can be seen at the far left of the image, while the more prominent edifice on the right belongs to whisky distillers John Dewar & Sons, who have had a presence in Perth since 1846. Prior to the Grouping in 1923, this was Caledonian Railway territory.

Stanley Junction, seven miles north of Perth, is where the ex-Highland Railway tracks branched off the former Caledonian Railway main line, which continued to Forfar and Aberdeen. The latter closed as a through route on 4 September 1967, although a goods service was maintained as far as Forfar until 5 June 1982. Seen here on 18 July 1988, keeping to the 35 mph speed restriction as it passes the former junction, Class 47 No. 47593 *Galloway Princess* (sporting InterCity colours) prepares to join the double-track section to Perth with 'The Clansman', the 10.35 service from Inverness to London Euston. Originally numbered D1973 when built in November 1965, the loco was then renumbered 47272 from September 1974, becoming 47593 in August 1983 when it was fitted with electric train heating equipment. The flat-topped signal box dated from 1962, the previous box being located in the 'V' between the Highland line, which veers to the left, and the Forfar route. The station at Stanley closed on 11 June 1956.

Opposite: Looking in the opposite direction on the same day, a small gang of track maintenance men pause to watch the progress (although at least one continues shovelling) of Class 47 No. 47541 *The Queen Mother* with the 11.35 from Edinburgh to Inverness, as it is about to enter the single-line section to Dunkeld. In the northbound direction speed was limited to 45 mph. The loco was ScotRail branded but retained the red stripe along the lower body sides from its InterCity days rather than the blue of ScotRail. Both locos on these two pages have three-piece snowploughs attached and are still extant – No. 47593 owned by Locomotive Services based at Crewe and No. 47541 by Vintage Trains at Tyseley, Birmingham.

On a soggy Thursday, 10 July 1986, a dozen passengers greet the arrival of Class 47 No. 47643 at Dunkeld with the 08.30 from Inverness to Bristol, where it was due to arrive at 19.52. On Fridays the train continued to Plymouth with a scheduled arrival time of 22.21. The station is actually in the village of Birnam; the cathedral 'city' of Dunkeld, with a population of some 1,300 souls, is on the opposite side of the River Tay. During the 1980s the station was known simply as Dunkeld, but was renamed Dunkeld and Birnam on 13 May 1991, Birnam having featured on the running-in boards in earlier years. The station architecture, canopy and footbridge are all worthy of study. In contrast the down platform is devoid of even the most basic facility.

On the same day at Dunkeld, fellow Class 47 No. 47642 *Strathisla* heads north with the 09.23 service from Edinburgh. All passenger trains calling at Dunkeld normally use the up platform as in this instance, which saves passengers a trek over the footbridge, unless there is a need to use the passing loop. While waiting for this train the signalman kindly offered the author some welcome shelter in the signal box (see overleaf).

Left: An interior view of Dunkeld signal box. On the shelf above the twenty-three lever frame (supplied by McKenzie & Holland in 1919) are the block telegraph instruments by which the signalman liaised with his colleagues in the boxes at Stanley Junction and Ballinluig. Tokenless block had been introduced along the route in 1968/69, the system ensuring the safe operation of the relevant single line sections. At roof level is a track diagram. A few carefully tended plants on the windowsill add to the ambience.

Below: North of Dunkeld, with the line having crossed the Highland Boundary Fault (the demarcation between the Highlands and Lowlands of Scotland), the scenery becomes more grand, as illustrated in this brief glimpse of a blue-liveried Class 47 dashing north along the fertile Strath of Tay at Dalguise on 11 April 1985.

High Speed Train power car No. 43107 *City of Derby* (with a second power car at the rear) hurries by the closed station at Ballinluig with the 12.00 'Highland Chieftain' service from London King's Cross, due to reach Inverness at 20.42 on 9 July 1986. During its 581-mile journey it stopped at fifteen stations on its way north. The HST power cars constructed at Crewe Works, utilising a 2,250hp Paxman Valenta engine, were introduced to the East Coast main line from 1978. From May 1984 one HST diagram was extended north of Edinburgh to Inverness, the set returning south early the next morning. North of Edinburgh it was not possible to exploit the full potential of the HSTs' 125 mph capability, although later some track modifications allowed 100 mph running over certain sections. Ballinluig, twenty-four miles north of Perth, was the junction for the eight and three-quarter mile branch to Aberfeldy, which closed on 3 May 1965, Ballinluig residents being deprived of their station on the same day. From Perth the railway has never been far away from the Tay, but just south of Ballinluig the river turns to the west towards Aberfeldy and Loch Tay. From Ballinluig as far as Pitlochry the Highland line follows the course of the River Tummel. *Inset*: A carriage window label detailing the stopping places of the 'Highland Chieftain' on its way north.

Class 47 No. 47469 *Glasgow Chamber of Commerce* passes the engineers' sidings at Ballinluig with the 12.20 from Inverness to Glasgow Queen Street on 12 April 1985. Part of Ballinluig village is visible on the opposite side of the A9 road. At first sight the large sign by the roadside can appear misleading, in that Aberfeldy and Killin along the A827 are west of here, the link road sweeping round to cross the railway by the bridge on which the author is standing. The loco has a West Highland terrier emblem on the body side, as applied by Eastfield depot (Glasgow) to its stock, where it enjoyed two periods of activity from April 1976 to May 1978 and October 1984 to January 1987. It was withdrawn in March 1989 due to collision damage while attached to Inverness depot.

Class 47 No. 47633 with large BR double-arrow logo and numerals, in charge of the 16.30 from Inverness to Glasgow, accelerates away from Pitlochry on a sunny 9 July 1986. Standing proud above the trees is the Atholl Palace Hotel near the centre of Pitlochry. The loco had assumed its current identity the previous December when, as the former No. D1668 (later No. 47083), it was modified to enable haulage of electric heated stock. It was condemned in November 1990.

Passengers prepare to board the southbound 'Highland Chieftain' led by No. 43198, the last of the HST power cars delivered to BR in August 1982, as it arrives at Pitlochry bound for King's Cross on 11 July 1987. Starting from Inverness at 07.50 the train had covered eighty-nine miles of its journey to the capital. Note the ornate drinking fountain by the main station building (see page 3) and the distinctive shelter on the down platform, much appreciated by travellers on less clement days.

The previous day another English Electric Vulcan Foundry product, Class 40 No. 40152 (originally No. D352, completed in July 1961), nears Pitlochry from the north with a mixed consist of wagons.

Class 37 No. 37237 powers away from Pitlochry with a rake of Presflo cement hoppers loaded at Blue Circle's Oxwellmains works, near Dunbar east of Edinburgh, for discharge at Inverness on 17 June 1980. Pitlochry signal box at the north end of the down platform is in view above the leading wagons. The loco was released from the English Electric Vulcan Foundry at Newton-le-Willows, Lancashire, as No. D6937 in May 1964.

Class 40 No. 40162 has just emerged from the north end of the tunnel and passes the site of the closed (3 May 1965) Killiecrankie station with a service linking the Scottish capital and Inverness on 17 June 1980. There was a passing loop and signal box here until 22 December 1963.

In the Pass of Killiecrankie, three and a half miles north of Pitlochry, No. 47469 *Glasgow Chamber of Commerce* crosses the deep ravine by this ten-arch stone viaduct with the 13.25 Edinburgh-Inverness service on 11 April 1985. Note the check rails on the viaduct. Below the author is the entrance to a 128-yards-long tunnel.

The Birmingham Railway Carriage & Wagon Company Type 2 Bo-Bos, fitted with 1,160hp Sulzer engines and with a maximum speed of 75 mph, were introduced from July 1958. By the summer of 1962, twenty-nine of the forty-seven built were allocated to Inverness depot. A further batch of sixty-nine with various modifications, including an uprated 1,250hp engine and able to reach 90 mph, were constructed by BRCW from June 1961. As Classes 26 and 27 respectively, all were based in Scotland by 1970. Here No. 27066, which had started life as No. D5386 in May 1962, nears Blair Atholl with a northbound freight, including petroleum tanks and wagons carrying domestic coal, on 12 April 1985. Subsequently preserved following withdrawal by BR in July 1987, the loco is now housed at Barrow Hill Railway Centre, near Chesterfield.

Opposite: Adorned with a large BR double-arrow logo and numerals, Class 47 No. 47617 *University of Stirling* hauls the 12.20 Inverness to Glasgow service away from Blair Atholl (the station is hidden by the tree on the left) and over the River Tilt on 11 April 1985. The painted stonework on the bridge support is to aid sighting of the semaphore signal by drivers of northbound trains. The loco entered traffic in May 1964 as No. D1742 (No. 47149 from February 1974), before being identified as No. 47617 from July 1984 after the installation of electric train heating equipment. It was retired in January 1998 and cut-up the next month.

Below: The following day No. 47620 leaves the lattice girder bridge spanning the Tilt, heading northbound with the 09.25 departure from Edinburgh. The castellated stone towers and archways of the bridge were added at the behest of the 6th Duke of Atholl; twenty-four miles of the route pass through the Atholl Estate. The entrance to the ancestral castle, famed for its private army, is located a short walk north of the station. New from Crewe Works as No. D1654 in February 1965, the loco led a fairly uneventful life under various guises until May 1995 when it was one of two locos chosen for Royal Train duties, renumbered 47799 and named *Prince Henry*. In October 1997, under EWS management following Privatisation, it was painted Royal Claret with red and gold stripes and given an EIIR emblem and crown on the body sides. After retirement from main line service in February 2004, this celebrity loco was saved from the cutter's torch and is now based at the Eden Valley Railway at Warcop in Cumbria.

Opposite: Working in multiple, Class 27s Nos. 27026 and 27059 run by the up platform at Blair Atholl with empty bitumen tanks while returning from Culloden to Ellesmere Port on 11 April 1985. When the station building was completed in 1869 a private waiting room for the Duke was provided at the south end, this wing last being used in 1963 before demolition. The station became unstaffed on 11 July 1983. Note the ex-Highland Railway goods shed behind the locos and, to the left, the former engine shed. In steam days locos were out-stationed here from Perth, principally to provide assistance to northbound trains, the line climbing from near 400 feet to 1,484 feet above sea level over the next eighteen miles to Druimuachdar Summit. Gradients are as steep as 1-in-70. Both locos emerged from the Birmingham Railway Carriage & Wagon Works at Smethwick in 1962 as Nos. D5372 and D5410 respectively. They survived in BR ownership until July 1987, and while the former was scrapped, No. 27059 was purchased by Sandwell Borough Council, the BRCW factory having been located in the borough. Normally it now resides on the Severn Valley Railway at Kidderminster, not too far from its birthplace.

Below: Two of the earlier slightly less powerful BRCW locos (see page 19) built in 1959, Nos. 26012 and 26029 in charge of a northbound coal train wait for the road ahead to clear, as the driver reminds the Blair Atholl signalman of his presence on 17 June 1980. The roof of the old engine shed is partially visible above the rear brake van. The train had been recessed in the sidings by the engine shed so as not to impede the following 13.10 Glasgow to Inverness passenger service. The twenty-four miles between Blair Atholl and Dalwhinnie were originally doubled in stages between 1900 and 1909, but were singled with a passing loop at Dalnacardoch in July 1966, only for the double track formation to be reinstated in April 1978. The two locos were withdrawn in January 1982 and October 1988 respectively.

As a prelude to Privatisation, from 1987 BR was split into various business sectors. Wearing Parcels Sector red and grey, Class 47 No. 47634 *Holbeck* powers 'The Clansman' up the 1-in-70 gradient at Dalnacardoch on 24 August 1991. Composed of InterCity liveried stock, the train had left London Euston at 07.35 that morning behind an ac electric locomotive, *Holbeck* having taken over at Mossend yard, south of Coatbridge. The remains of the signal box that controlled the passing loop at this location from 1966 until double-track was restored in 1978, is visible above the third coach. *Inset*: A carriage window label detailing the stopping places of the corresponding southbound 'Clansman' in 1985.

Two English Electric Vulcan Foundry-built 1,750hp Class 37s, Nos. 37035 and 37261 *Caithness*, drift downhill at Dalnacardoch on 11 July 1989 with an afternoon Speedlink service from the north conveying empty coal containers, discharged cement hoppers, LPG tanks and loaded timber. Note the emergency crossover between the up and down lines and the A9 road in the middle distance. In total 242 of these versatile locos were put together at the maker's Vulcan factory at Newton-le-Willows in Lancashire, and a further sixty-seven at their former Robert Stephenson & Hawthorns plant in Darlington. While No. 37035 no longer exists, its companion remains in Scotland at the heritage Bo'ness & Kinneil Railway, West Lothian.

Amid the bleak terrain of the Pass of Druimuachdar, Class 26 No. 26045 confidently climbs towards the summit of the line – at 1,484 feet above sea level now the highest in Britain – with half-a-dozen empty ballast hoppers on 17 June 1980. Completed as No. D5345 in October 1959, the loco had a brief sojourn at Haymarket (Edinburgh) before spending rest of its career attached to Inverness depot. It was withdrawn in July 1983.

Soon after passing the summit, Haymarket-based Class 40 No. 40158 coasts downgrade near Dalnaspidal as it heads for home with the 09.45 service from Inverness on 16 June 1980. The loco arrived new at the Edinburgh depot in September 1961, staying there until May 1981 when it was moved to Carlisle, where it spent its last days before withdrawal in December 1983.

Class 47 No. 47704 *Dunedin* hurries non-stop through the village of Dalwhinnie, having just entered the double track section to Blair Atholl while heading to Glasgow with the 16.33 from Inverness on 8 September 1990. The signal box is partially visible behind the stone building at the end of the platform. At an altitude of 1,174 feet above sea level, Dalwhinnie is the highest main line station in Britain.

On 16 July 1983, after passing Dalwhinnie station, No. 47546 continues north along the single track towards Inverness with 'The Clansman', the 09.30 from Euston (departure time from London varied over the years). Prominent is the 1898-established Dalwhinnie Distillery, famed for its single malt whisky. As an Inverness allocated loco and frequently passing this way, it was appropriately named *Aviemore Centre* in May 1985, a name it retained until its death-knell was sounded in 1999.

From Dalwhinnie to Newtonmore, a distance of ten miles, the railway threads Glen Truim. Here Class 47 No. 47578 nears Dalwhinnie with the 16.30 departure from Inverness, en route to the Scottish capital on 16 July 1983. The loco remained in service until March 2004 after an active life of forty years.

Earlier on the same day, in a narrower part of the glen at Crubenmore, with the River Truim on the left flowing north towards its confluence with the Spey just south of Newtonmore, No. 47207 makes steady progress on the climb towards Dalwhinnie with the 10.20 service from Inverness to Scotland's second city. This Crewe-built loco was aged thirty-five when withdrawn in April 2001.

On the same day as the pictures opposite, No. 47464 prepares to stop at Newtonmore while on its way south to Glasgow, having left Inverness at 12.30. Except for the Class 08 shunters, numerically the 47s were the largest class of locos ordered by BR, with 512 built over five years from September 1962, the Brush Falcon Works at Loughborough being responsible for 310 with 202 built at BR's own workshops at Crewe. They had Sulzer engines initially rated at 2,750hp, but which from 1966 were derated to 2,580hp; they had a Co-Co wheel arrangement and a maximum speed of 95 mph. Over the years members of the class were the subject of various modifications. No. 47464 was released from Crewe Works in May 1964 as No. D1587, and as an example fitted with electric train heating equipment was renumbered 47464 under the TOPS computer system in December 1973. The loco was condemned in October 1986 at the comparatively young age of twenty-two years. The previous year in April 1985, the loop, sidings and attendant signal box at Newtonmore were dispensed with and the station building which had served since Highland Railway days was subsequently sold. Today all that remains is a basic shelter for waiting passengers.

A couple of vehicles wait patiently for the level crossing barriers to lift at the north end of Kingussie station on 14 April 1990, as Class 47 No. 47617 *University of Stirling* clatters onto the girder bridge spanning the Gynack Burn, which flows into the Spey to the left of the picture. The train, including sleeping cars, had left London Euston at 22.15 the previous evening. The loco sports InterCity colours, having had a repaint since seen at Blair Atholl in April 1985 (see page 20). Based at Inverness, during the summer of 1991 it was among seven Class 47s to have its electric train heating capacity increased for use on sleeper services. To readily distinguish the locos concerned they were renumbered in the 4767X series, *University of Stirling* becoming No. 47677.

Following a light dusting of snow, HST power car No. 43058 leads the 'Highland Chieftain', the 08.00 from Inverness to London King's Cross, as it arrives at Kingussie on 16 April 1990. No. 43058 was built by British Rail Engineering Ltd at Crewe for East Coast main line services in July 1977. Today it is owned by Locomotive Services based at Crewe.

Against a backdrop of the Cairngorms, famous for its ski slopes, Class 47 No. 47171 gathers speed soon after departing from Aviemore with the 17.10 from Inverness, en route to Edinburgh on Sunday 13 June 1982. In the foreground is the old A9 road, now the B9152 between Aviemore and Kingussie. The loco had strayed far from its Cardiff Canton home, where it was domiciled between November 1974 and October 1987. Retired at the end of 2000, it was early 2003 before it was cut-up, the only Class 47 to suffer the fate in the yard of S. Norton of Liverpool, although one cab survives in The Cab Yard as part of a private collection in South Wales.

Opposite: Class 47 No. 47541 *The Queen Mother* waits at Aviemore platform 1, the most convenient for the main entrance, with the 12.30 Inverness to Glasgow service on 14 April 1990. Platform 3 on the right, occupied by wagons and machines for permanent-way work, has been utilised by the neighbouring Strathspey Railway since July 1998. In its earlier years from August 1964 the loco roamed the Western, London Midland and Eastern regions before emigrating to Scotland in January 1978. The nameplates were unveiled by HM The Queen Mother herself during a ceremony at Aberdeen station on 20 October 1982. It was based at Inverness from October 1984 until November 1990, and proudly wears the depot's Highland Rail stag's head emblem on the body side (see page 52). Withdrawn by EWS in February 2004, it was later purchased by Vintage Trains of Tyseley, Birmingham, in March 2007 and has continued to work on the main line network from time to time.

The heritage Strathspey Railway was born in 1972 following the purchase of five miles of track between Aviemore and Boat of Garten. Originally part of the Highland Railway main line to Inverness via Grantown-on-Spey and Forres, it was closed to passengers on 18 October 1965, although the track as far as Boat of Garten continued to be used for goods until 4 November 1968. The Strathspey inaugurated public services on 22 July 1978, but with access to Aviemore station not possible until July 1998; in the interim a new platform known as Aviemore Speyside was provided some 300 yards north of the BR station. Here, on 13 April 1990, Stanier 'Black 5' 4-6-0 No. 5025 arrives from Boat of Garten, as ballast is slowly released from the hopper behind Class 27 Bo-Bo No. D5394. The two locos represent classes that in earlier eras were a familiar sight on the main line at Aviemore. In fact, No. 5025 was among the first batch of ten 'Black 5s' built for the LMS at Vulcan Foundry, Newton-le-Willows, Lancashire, in August/September 1934, that were allocated to Perth when new. It was first noted in the north on 5 September 1934 at the head of the 12.12pm Perth to Inverness via Forres service. It left Perth in October 1935 and spent the rest of its LMS and subsequent BR days at English sheds, remaining active until the very end of regular steam traction on BR in August 1968. Earlier, at the end of 1960 when BR stopped keeping detailed records, No. 5025 had clocked 1,007,940 miles. The main line towards Inverness is on the left, while out of sight on the right is the ex-Highland Railway Aviemore engine shed, coded 60B in BR days with an allocation of up to a dozen locos, including 'Black 5s', before closure at the end of 1962. The shed is now utilised by the Strathspey Railway.

In pristine condition, wearing its original green livery with a white stripe around the body and BR crest, recent newcomer to the Strathspey Railway No. D5394 looks on as Hunslet 'Austerity' 0-6-0ST No. 60 approaches Boat of Garten from Aviemore on 17 July 1988. Constructed by the Birmingham Railway Carriage & Wagon Company, No. D5394 spent its infant years from June 1962 on the London Midland Region, before moving to Scotland in July 1968. It was then attached to Eastfield depot prior to allocation to Inverness from August 1981 until May 1986, before being retired from Eastfield as No. 27050 in July 1987. The steam loco has a very different pedigree. Built to a wartime design by the Hunslet Engine Company of Leeds for the National Coal Board in 1948, as NCB No. 60 it was utilised on a number of colliery railways in County Durham, before being transported from Dawdon Colliery, Seaham, to the Strathspey in July 1976. It has since returned to England and is now on the stock list of the Aln Valley Railway at Alnwick, Northumberland. Also worthy of note is Boat of Garten South signal box and the attendant mechanical signalling.

Opposite: Despite the rain and being far from its early Caledonian Railway metals, McIntosh '812' class 0-6-0 No. 828, restored to its 1899 condition, positively sparkles in its blue livery at Boat of Garten as it prepares to leave for Aviemore on 10 September 1993. Seventy-nine of these elegant locos were built in 1899/1900, twenty-nine in the Caledonian Railway's workshops at St Rollox in Glasgow (including No. 828), with the remainder by outside contractors. Under the LMS, following the Grouping in 1923 the engines began to stray from their previous home territory, with some reaching the Highlands. In BR days Aviemore was home to classmate No. 57586 from January 1949 until it was declared as surplus in June 1961, while others were resident for short periods. Ten of the class survived into 1963, among them No. 828 which had become BR No. 57566 by the time of its withdrawal from Ardrossan shed in August of that year. It is the only member of the class still in existence.

Right: With an admiring audience of both young and old, No. 5025 rolls into Boat of Garten from Aviemore on 15 April 1990. On the opposite platform at this picturesque location, the running-in board (seen above the tender) reads 'Boat of Garten Change for Speyside Line' – the former Great North of Scotland Railway route to Craigellachie. This closed to passengers on 18 October 1965, the same day services were discontinued to Forres. Contrasting motive power resting by the station sign is Andrew Barclay 0-4-0ST works No. 2020, built at the company's Kilmarnock works in 1936. The saddle tank previously worked the privately-owned one-and-a-half-mile branch to Balmenach Distillery from the Great North of Scotland line at Cromdale, near Grantown-on-Spey. It was donated to the Strathspey by Scottish Malt Distillers. Since 31 May 2002 Strathspey Railway trains have continued to Broomhill, a further five miles along the 'old road' towards Inverness, with the aim of eventually restoring the line as far as Grantown-on-Spey.

Below: A closer view of the Andrew Barclay loco taken at Boat of Garten on 13 June 1982.

Back at Aviemore, passengers aboard the 09.23 from Edinburgh behind No. 47591 enjoy a brief sight of Ivatt Class 2 2-6-0 No. 46464, resting on the Strathspey Railway turntable, as they head towards Inverness on 12 July 1987. The turntable was previously used at Kyle of Lochalsh. The 'Mogul' was released from Crewe Works in June 1950 and apart from short spells attached to the sheds at St Margarets (Edinburgh) and Kittybrewster (Aberdeen), spent the vast majority of its BR days allocated to Dundee Tay Bridge, before being withdrawn in August 1966. The Class 47 was also a product of Crewe, launched as No. D1965 in October 1965, and like its elder steam counterpart still survives, back at Crewe with Locomotive Services.

With long distances involved for many people wanting to travel to the north of Scotland, some motorists were happy to take advantage of the now-discontinued Motorail services. Here, with a couple of cars secured on the wagons at the rear of the 14.48 Inverness to Glasgow service, No. 47431 rolls into Carrbridge on 12 June 1980. The Class 47 was far from home, being on the books of Finsbury Park depot (London) during the summer of 1980, having gone north earlier in the day with the 09.45 from Edinburgh. Indeed the loco led a somewhat peripatetic existence, for after beginning life as No. D1545 at Darnall depot (Sheffield) in October 1963, it moved the short distance to Tinsley in May 1964, where it would eventually be allocated for five separate periods. It also resided at Bescot, was twice placed on the register maintained by Crewe, as well as Finsbury Park (3), Gateshead (2), Haymarket, Immingham (2), March, the Nottingham and Stoke divisions, Stratford (London) and York (4), before its active days were ended at Old Oak Common (London) in July 1992. In total the engine was transferred between depots on twenty-five occasions during its career.

Edinburgh Haymarket-based English Electric 2,000hp Class 40 No. 40165 powers away from the passing loop at Carrbridge station, heading north to Inverness with the 13.10 service from Glasgow on 12 June 1980. Haymarket was the only Scottish depot to have an allocation of these heavy 1Co-Co1 locos; they turned the scales at 133 tons but had a maximum speed of 90 mph. A total of 200, numbered D200 to D399, entered service between March 1958 and September 1962, 180 emerging from the English Electric Vulcan Foundry works at Newton-le-Willows in Lancashire and twenty from the former Robert Stephenson & Hawthorns plant at Darlington. Haymarket received seven new from Vulcan Foundry in February/March 1960 and a further twelve from the same source during the second half of 1961, among the latter batch No. 40165 as No. D365 in November 1961; these were regularly employed over the Highland main line to Inverness. At the start of 1980 Haymarket had responsibility for twenty-six of these venerable locos, but their time in Scotland was drawing to a close; numbers then declined rapidly, with the remaining eight moving south to England in October 1981. No. 40165 had been condemned at Haymarket the previous July.

Opposite: On the same day, soon after passing Carrbridge, Class 27 No. 27005 rides above the River Dulnain, northbound with a mixed freight consisting of at least four mineral wagons and a couple of oil tanks, the latter destined for Lairg. A further five miles of climbing lie ahead to Slochd Summit, much of it at 1-in-60. New to Eastfield shed (Glasgow) as No. D5351 in August 1961, the loco moved to Inverness in March 1980 before returning to Eastfield in May 1986. In July 1987 BR decided it had no further use for the loco, though happily the next year it was saved from the clutches of a scrap merchant and remains in Scotland on the stock list of the Bo'ness & Kinneil Railway in West Lothian.

Having surmounted the 1,315-foot summit at Slochd one and a half miles back, Class 47 No. 47533 leads six coaches off the eight-arch masonry Slochd Viaduct with the 16.50 from Inverness to Glasgow on 13 July 1986. This Crewe-built loco served BR for twenty-six years prior to its demise in June 1991.

A Class 37 climbs the 1-in-60 gradient across the impressive Findhorn Viaduct, near Tomatin, with nine empty tanks as it returns south from the Highland Bitumen sidings at Culloden (see page 49) on 12 July 1984. The meandering River Findhorn can be seen below the 445-yards-long nine-span viaduct, the steelwork held aloft by solid masonry supports.

Opposite: Looking very smart in blue livery, with wrap-around yellow ends, large logo and numerals, and further embellished by the Highland Rail stag's head emblem by the driver's door (see page 52), No. 37261 *Caithness* hauls a short rake of empty wagons of various descriptions south near Tomatin on 11 July 1986. This was a pleasant spot to while away the time on a sunny morning such as this, but there's little doubt members of the track maintenance gang welcomed the shelter of the corrugated tin-roofed hut in the foreground during the harsh conditions often experienced in these parts. From new in January 1967, this Class 37 served the Eastern Region until April 1982, when it was transferred north from Stratford depot (London) to Eastfield (Glasgow), before moving the next month to Inverness. The name *Caithness*, Scotland's most northerly mainland region, was conferred on the loco in May 1985. While based at Inverness it rubbed shoulders with No. 27005 (see page 42), and today the pair remain companions at the Bo'ness & Kinneil Railway.

Below: A ScotRail Class 47, painted in InterCity colours (the small numerals applied with this livery often made positive identification difficult), needs all its available 2,580hp as it heaves the 19.30 sleeper service upgrade from Inverness on 13 July 1986. The heavy train, fourteen miles into its 587 miles overnight journey to London Euston, where it was due to arrive at 06.49, is crossing the Grade A listed timber Aultnaslanach Viaduct, near Moy. From here by road it is only eight miles to the centre of Inverness, the railway tracing a longer but much easier route, initially in the direction of Nairn along Drummossie Muir.

In order to cross the wide valley of the River Nairn at Culloden, the Highland Railway constructed a 600-yard-long viaduct of red sandstone, the line hereabouts turning through 180 degrees over a couple of miles, as it continues its descent towards Inverness. Here with Culloden Forest below the skyline, beyond which the land falls away towards the Moray Firth, Class 47 No. 47040 hurries from the viaduct in charge of the 12.20 from Inverness to Glasgow on 11 July 1984. The loco was taken out of service in March 2000 and subsequently scrapped.

Opposite: On the same day fellow Class 47 No. 47209, pulling some loaded mineral wagons, has just entered the double track section by Culloden Moor station (closed 3 May 1965), for the remaining six miles to Inverness. As is evident from the width of the viaduct, the double track formation previously extended further south, the four-mile length as far as Daviot being singled on 31 March 1968. To the left of the signal box a road tanker is in process of collecting bitumen for road surfacing work from the Highland Bitumen sidings. Like its classmate above, No. 47209 was a product of Crewe Works, but when its usefulness as a Class 47 expired in September 2002 it was later taken to Brush Traction at Loughborough for rebuilding as a Class 57. It was outshopped with a General Motors 2,750hp engine as No. 57604 *Pendennis Castle* in January 2004 and remains part of a small fleet operated by Great Western Railway.

English Electric Class 37 No. 37431 leaves Inverness behind with the 10.15 service to Edinburgh on 11 September 1993. As an aid to flexible working over the section from Millburn Junction, southbound trains were able to use either line to this point. The bulbs on the angled bracket on the colour-light signal would have been lit, indicating the train was to cross over to the up line just behind the author. The milepost by the foot of the signal confirms the distance from Perth to be 116¾ miles. Above the loco, and where the waters of the Beauly Firth flow into the Moray Firth, is Kessock Bridge which carries the A9 road onto the Black Isle. No. 37431 was retained in main line service for a further six years, before being condemned in December 1999.

Opposite: Travelling in the opposite direction towards Inverness at the same location on 13 June 1980 are Class 20s Nos. 20156 and 20152 with LPG tanks bound for the British Aluminium smelter at Invergordon. The single line at a lower level on the left is that from Aberdeen; this was also used by trains from Perth prior to the completion of the route over Slochd. The two lines merge at Millburn Junction. English Electric delivered 228 of these locomotives to BR between June 1957 and February 1968. They became a familiar sight in and around Inverness from the winter of 1960 when three were allocated to the depot for freight duties, although the last were transferred away in February 1980. These two examples, as Nos. D8156 and D8152 respectively, were based from new in August 1966 on the London Midland Region, both having moved north to Haymarket depot in Edinburgh in May 1980. No. 20152 was withdrawn in April 1988 and No. 20156 in June 1991.

With the impending demise of steam in the north of Scotland, the former Highland Railway Lochgorm locomotive works by the side of Inverness station were closed in July 1959. By the following summer the site had been refurbished as a diesel maintenance depot, the 60A code of its steam predecessor being retained. By October 1960 the new facility had become home to fifty diesel locomotives, the stock consisting of forty-one Type 2s with Sulzer 1,160hp engines, nineteen built by BR at Derby Works and twenty-two by the Birmingham Railway Carriage and Wagon Company (later Classes 24 and 26 respectively), three English Electric Type 1s (later Class 20), and six shunting locos – five Andrew Barclay 204hp 0-4-0s and one BR-built 350hp 0-6-0 (later Class 08). Twenty years later, at the start of 1980, the depot, then known by the letters IS, had forty-four locos on its books – four Class 08s, three Class 20s, thirty-one Class 26s and six Class 47s. By 1990 the total number of locomotives had been reduced to twenty-four made up of three Class 08s, thirteen Class 37s and eight Class 47s, the shed also having charge of six Class 156 diesel multiple-units for use on the lines north of Inverness. Here, on Sunday 15 June 1980, having returned to its home depot after bringing north a sleeper service from London Euston, Class 47 No. 47472 has its fuel tanks replenished. The lines on the left are the Rose Street curve which links the routes to the south and north of the city, bypassing the station platforms. *Inset*: The Highland Rail stag's head emblem that adorned many IS allocated locomotives (see pages 35 and 46).

Opposite: On the same day two further home-based locomotives, Nos. 27108 and 26035, receive a weekend wash and brush-up. The Class 27 had only moved to Inverness in February 1980, while the Class 26 had graced the shed since June 1960 when just under one year old. The former was rendered extinct by scrap merchant Vic Berry of Leicester shortly after withdrawal in July 1987, while No. 26035 survives on the Caledonian Railway at Brechin near Montrose.

Inside Inverness depot, where the Highland Railway put together forty-one new steam locomotives between 1869 and 1906, Nos. 37262 *Dounreay* and 47630 undergo some routine maintenance work on 12 July 1986. Prominent 'Not to be Moved' notices hang from both locomotives. The Class 37 was allocated to Inverness in May 1982, while the Class 47 was a more recent arrival, having been transferred to the depot two months earlier. No. 37262 was named on 14 May 1985 during a ceremony at Thurso station, Dounreay Nuclear Power Station being a little further west along the north coast of Scotland. It was withdrawn in March 2000 and No. 47630 followed a year later, neither locomotive escaping the cutter's torch.

During the early 1980s Inverness depot had three diagrams for the Class 08s. Duties included hauling empty coaching stock in and out of the station, as well as shunting and transferring goods wagons between the various yards. Here, No. 08568 awaits its next move at the goods depot by the side of the station on 11 July 1984. The locomotive was a product of Crewe Works as No. D3735 in April 1959, and had been a familiar sight around Inverness since 1960. Today the loco lives on as part of a fleet of ex-BR Class 08s owned by Railway Support Services and available for hire.

Looking quite resplendent on the left, Class 47 No. 47550 *University of Dundee* awaits departure time before leaving with the 12.30 to Glasgow on 15 July 1989. On the right by the south wall of the diesel depot, and looking equally smart, Class 37 No. 37418 *An Comunn Gaidhealach* has charge of the 'Royal Scotsman' luxury train during a grand tour of Scottish lines. The platforms used by trains for Kyle of Lochalsh, Wick and Thurso, at right angles to those pictured, are hidden by the coaching stock. Unlike No. 47550, which was condemned in September 1996, No. 37418 still survives and is now owned by Colas Rail Freight.